MW01517647

Colonial Inspirations

*Silk ribbon and lace designs
for New Zealanders*

Beverley Sheldrick

David Bateman

Acknowledgements

I would like to thank my friend Elizabeth who, over the years, has become my third eye; Justine for her faith in asking me to write this book and her constant encouragement and patience; Maryfrances for her deciphering of my notes, typing them and patiently listening to my descriptions; Michael for all his help with and taking of the photographs; my husband who continues to love me despite all my artistic ups and downs.

Published in 1994 by David Bateman Ltd, 'Golden Heights',
32–34 View Road, Glenfield, Auckland, New Zealand
Reprinted 1995

North American Distributor:
Quilters' Resource Inc.
P.O. Box 148850
Chicago, IL. 60614
Phone: 312-278-5695

ISBN 1 86953 181 7

Cover design Chris O'Brien/Pages Literary Pursuits
Photography Michael Jeans, Cambridge
Word processing Maryfrances Wells
Art work Pali Pancha
Typeset in 12/13.5 Perpetua
Printed in Hong Kong by Colorcraft

Contents

Introduction

Most people have no difficulty mastering the embroidery or lace techniques. What they do find difficult is knowing where to put the various flowers, buds, leaves, etc. In this book I have looked to the past for my inspiration and in some cases, as in the bow design, I have used the same design in a number of ways; by shrinking or stretching, I have moulded it to fit the object. I love bows, and the shape of this particular bow came from the copper cover over the little fireplace in my bedroom.

When I first started searching for ideas, I looked at the type of objects our forebears embroidered and this has influenced my choice of items. We don't always realise how bright the colours they used in their embroideries were, hence the very strong colours used in the cushion, pillow and blouse. Leafing through a book of 18th-century silk fabric designs, I was struck by a simple violet motif. While the design on the blouse has been altered considerably from the original, nevertheless it was the starting point.

My favourite design is the dear little garland on one of the spectacles cases. My husband found this for me in the front of a book dated 1823. It was very suitable for silk ribbons and again I have copied it as closely as possible.

I love to work with natural fabrics and never mind the cost because:

a) they are so easy to work with;

b) they are so comfortable to wear; and

c) I save every little scrap and use them in the type of small projects featured in this book.

Many of the items in this book can be easily made by beginners, and make wonderful gifts of love. (There is a glossary on page 9 giving meanings for some specialist terms used, and these have been italicised in the text.) The more advanced pieces, for example the hussif, are so pretty they make the time and effort worthwhile.

I hope you have as much pleasure making some of these items as I have had designing them, and that you too will feel encouraged to try to capture some of the beauty of the designs that inspired our grandmothers.

Beverley Sheldrick

Fabrics

I prefer to use pure fabrics, such as linen and *Swiss batiste*, and save all the small leftover scraps from dressmaking. Fabrics made from natural fibres are much easier to work with and I also find the better quality laces give a far better finish and, again, I save all the small leftover pieces.

Silk ribbon

I use pure silk ribbon for the embroidery. It is impossible to give precise measurements for each of the projects, but I find 2 m is a good length to buy. Once you start doing silk ribbon embroidery, you quickly accumulate small pieces. Always work with a 30 cm length or less. I have used 4-mm ribbon in most of the projects, with a little 7-mm ribbon in some. In my instructions I give the number of shades required, but it is up to you to choose the actual colour you want.

NB: If using strongly coloured ribbon, soak it in cold salty water for about half an hour and iron dry before using. This sets the colour. I have worn and hand-washed my blouses over several years and have never had any problems with them.

Stiffenings

I find plastic ice-cream containers make excellent bases, e.g., in the heart pin cushion and the toilet bag. By using plastic in these items they are able to be washed, which would not be possible if you used cardboard. I prefer iron-on fusings for facings, etc.

Transferring designs

For marking designs I use a blue dressmaker's marker pen. Using this pen, trace the embroidery design onto the fabric. If the fabric is opaque, hold the design behind the fabric and tape both to a window. This acts as a 'light box'. It is **important** to immerse the work in **cold** water on completion of the embroidery to remove these markings. Once the blue pen has disappeared, place embroidery on a towel to remove excess water. Then, carefully peg to a coat hanger and hang in the shade to dry.

Some people use a disappearing marker, but although the marks disappear a residue remains on the fabric and can cause it to deteriorate at a later date, so I don't use this type of marker for heirloom sewing.

NB: The labels actual size, 80% actual size, 50% actual size, etc., indicate the enlargement necessary when photocopying the designs for transfer.

The stitches

Palestrina stitch

A double knot stitch which looks best worked in pearl cotton or *cotton à broder* to show texture to best advantage. Work from left to right. Make a straight stitch, then loop thread over and under as shown. Pull the needle through over top of working thread. Continue along line to be filled.

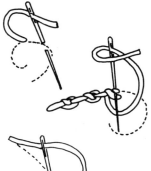

Stem stitch

Work from left to right, taking regular slightly slanting stitches along the line of the design, keeping the thread below the needle.

Chain stitch

Work chain stitch downwards, as shown in the diagram, by making a series of loops of identical size. Anchor the last loop with a tiny straight stitch.

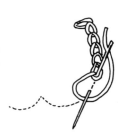

Straight stitch

Bring the needle out at one end and take it down again at the other end.

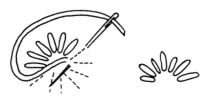

Slip stitch

This is an almost invisible stitch formed by slipping the thread under a fold of fabric. Work from right to left. Fasten thread and bring needle and thread out through one folded edge. For the first and each succeeding stitch, slip needle through fold of opposite edge for about 6 mm; bring needle out and draw the thread through.

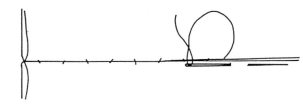

Pistil stitch

Bring needle up at A. Wrap thread once or twice around the needle. Go down at B (required distance from A), pulling thread taut around needle as it passes through the fabric.

French knots

These are a wonderful addition to any piece of work. If you have a gap, you can work a French knot and it becomes a bud. Bring the thread through the fabric and hold it taut with your left hand. Twist the thread around the needle 2 or 3 times and tighten. Still holding the thread in the left hand, turn the needle and insert into the fabric at the point where it originally emerged. Pull the needle and thread through the twists.

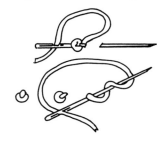

Buttonhole stitch

This is a looped line stitch which is often worked into a circle to form a daisy-type flower. It is worked from left to right, pulling the needle through the fabric over the top of the working thread. The closeness of each stitch depends on the flower.

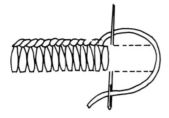

Straight stitch bud

Make a padded straight stitch, but do not pull tight. Anchor bud with a small straight stitch. Form leaves and stem with a fly stitch, using ribbon or embroidery thread.

Spider web rose

With embroidery thread, make a fly stitch. Add a bar of the same length on each side, giving 5 spokes. Using ribbon, come up in the centre of the spokes and begin weaving over and under them. Allow ribbon to twist and keep it loose. Continue until spokes are covered.

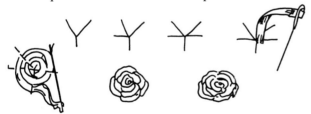

Ribbon stitch

Bring the needle up at point A and spread ribbon flat on fabric. Push the needle back through centre of ribbon at point B. Pull needle through to back of work very carefully as the finished shape of the petal or leaf depends on the ribbon just curling over at the tip.

Fly stitch

Each separate stitch looks like a capital 'Y'. Bring the needle through at the top left of the line to be covered and insert it diagonally back into the fabric, making a V-shaped loop as shown. Pull the needle through, over the working thread, and work a vertical straight stitch to hold the loop in place.

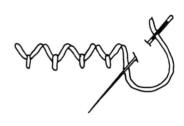

Lazy daisy stitch

This is actually a single chain stitch, but we have used it to form a flower, so shape it into a circle.

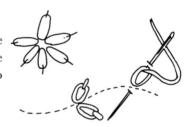

Lazy daisy rose

Come up at A and go down at B using a ribbon stitch. Come up at the base of this stitch and make a lazy daisy stitch angled to the right and another angled to the left. Go down at E. Use the darker shade of green to make the base of the rose, make a straight stitch angled to the right (tucked to the right of D). Lay a straight stitch along the outside of the left lazy daisy. The third stitch covers the base of the second straight stitch (along the right side of the left lazy daisy).

*H*eirloom techniques

The following are the basic methods used in heirloom sewing.

Stitch in the ditch (Fig. 1)

A line of machine stitching hard against the edge of *entredeux*.

Roll and whip (Fig. 2)

Cut away seam allowance leaving 2 mm.

Zigzag from stitch in the ditch to beyond the cut edge (Fig. 3). The stitch length is short, e.g., setting 0.8 or 1 on your sewing machine, and the width is approximately 4.5 or 5. This gives a very neat, strong edge.

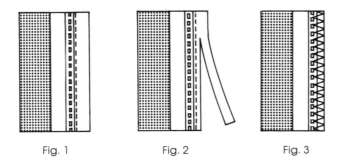

Fig. 1   Fig. 2   Fig. 3

Lace to lace (Fig. 4)

Butt the lace and zigzag together, stitch length 1, width 2.5. When starting, make sure the machine foot is sitting on both pieces of lace, otherwise it will just disappear into the feed dogs.

Fig. 4

Lace to entredeux (Fig. 5)

Trim waste away hard against heading on one side of the entredeux. Butt lace along this cut edge. Zigzag, approximate length 1, width 2.5, to ensure that the stitch goes into each hole of the entredeux and just over heading of the lace.

Shaping lace

Mark the design on the fabric. Then, taking care not to stretch the outer edge, carefully lie the lace over design and pin into place, concentrating on the outer edge and getting the lace lying flat. Use *lots* of lace pins and place them across the lace; the inner edge will pucker, but this will be corrected during the next step.

Spreading your fingers over the area to be shaped, carefully pull the outside thread in the lace heading on the inner edge. When pulling a loop, start at

Fig. 5

the bottom of the loop (or in the case of a bow, at the centre of the knot) and pull the thread as far as half way. Then start on the other inner edge and pull the other side. Adjust the gathers using your thumb nail.

When all is flat, lightly spray with starch and leave to dry. If you are worried the shape may be lost, you can tack the lace in place before sewing, otherwise it can be stitched to the fabirc using a small zigzag stitch (e.g., length 1, width 2.5). Stitch all the outer edges first, the needle falling just over the outer edge of the lace and then just over the heading. Be careful around the corners especially — don't try to hurry this job!

To flip the tails, simply fold the lace across itself to follow the line of the traced design.

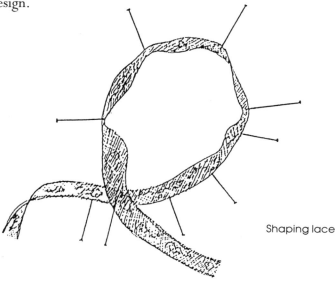

Shaping lace

Glossary

Batting   A padding fabric used in quilt-making. In this book it is used for covering coat hangers and for general padding, as in the tea cosy.

Beading lace   These are woven with a series of centre holes through which you can thread ribbon.

Cotton à broder   A tightly twisted thread similar to a fine weight of pearl cotton, but without the lustre.

Edging lace   This lace has one straight side and the other side has a definite border or scalloped edge.

Entredeux   Narrow, evenly woven beading used between two edges, giving a ladder-like effect. From the French word meaning 'between two'.

Insertion lace   A band of lace or embroidery with two straight edges and most of the strong gathering threads woven into each edge.

Pellen   A stabilising fabric used on the back of ribbon embroidery so the ribbon ends don't show through, especially on very fine fabric such as Swiss Batiste.

Pintuck   For the projects in this book, pintucking is done with a double needle and pintuck foot. Simply stitch along your guidelines; there is no need to fold the fabric. However, if you don't have a pintuck foot you can very carefully fold the fabric to achieve the same effect.

Swiss batiste   100% pure cotton fabric woven in Switzerland. This fabric is very fine and particularly suited to heirloom sewing.

*H*eart pin cushion

These lovely pin cushions were hung on the wall, often purely for decoration. The idea of the garland of roses was suggested by an old Victorian postcard.

Materials

- 2 pieces of fabric, 20 cm square
- 1 20-cm square of *pellen*
- 3 shades of pink silk ribbon — 2 m dark tone; 4 m medium tone; 6 m light tone
- 50 cm pale green silk ribbon
- 20 x 10 cm oblong of plastic (e.g., from an ice-cream container)
- 20 cm braid or ribbon for hanger
- 23 pins

actual size

1.   Using pattern provided on page 28, mark heart shape on both pieces of fabric. Cut pellen into 4 equal pieces. Tack one piece of pellen to the wrong side of each piece of fabric to be embroidered.

2.   Using the design above as a guide, mark the position of the roses.

3.   Work roses in spider web stitch (see page 7).

4.   Take the second piece of fabric and pellen and work single rose in spider web stitch using ribbon stitch for leaves and stem stitch for stem. Trim both pieces of pellen back to marked heart shape.

5.   Run a tacking thread around the edge of both pieces of fabric.

6.   Cut 2 pieces of plastic and pellen to the dotted line on the heart shape pattern.

7.   Place fabric right side down, add pellen, then plastic. Gently pull tacking thread to enclose plastic evenly, distributing folds. Knot firmly. Do the same to second piece.

8.   Fold a 20-cm piece of ribbon or cord in half and attach firmly to top of the heart.

9.   With wrong sides together, carefully slip stitch the two pieces together.

10.   Cover the seam with Palestrina stitch (see page 6) or ready-made braid. Insert pearl-headed pins at even intervals all the way around.

actual size

*E*ye shades *(bow design)*

We tend to think of these as a modern idea given to us by airline companies! However, our wealthy ancestors often suffered from attacks of the 'vapours' and shades would be worn to help one sleep.

Materials

- 10 x 20 cm main fabric
- 10 x 20 cm satin lining
- 2 pieces of *pellen* 10 x 20 cm
- 2.2 m *insertion lace*
- 80 cm elastic
- 50 cm *beading lace*
- 50 cm ribbon
- embroidery thread slightly darker than ribbon
- 55 cm piping

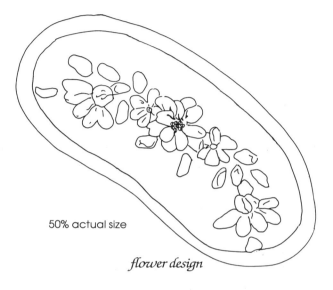

50% actual size

flower design

1. Using pattern provided (page 28), cut shape from silk, lining and 2 pieces of pellen.
2. Transfer design from page 32 onto silk with dressmaker's marker pen. Tack to pellen and then work design (shaping lace as described on pages 8–9 and decorating with French knots).
3. Stitch piping around outer edge.
4. Using nose pattern, cut 1 piece of silk and 1 of pellen. Tack around edge and across middle lengthwise. Fold in half, tack together edge to edge. Tack nose piece to shade as shown in diagram. This will need careful easing.

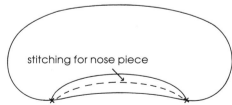

stitching for nose piece

5. Tack second piece of pellen to wrong side of satin lining.
6. Cut 2 pieces of elastic 37 cm long and 4 pieces of insertion lace 55 cm long. Using a zigzag stitch, join outer edges of laces together to form 2 tubes. Thread elastic through these tubes. Stitch to eye shades where indicated on pattern.
7. Following piping stitch line, and with right sides together, join lining to main fabric. Carefully stitch round outer edge leaving a gap of 6 cm at the top. Turn through and carefully hand stitch together.

*E*ye shades *(flower design)*

Extra materials
- silk ribbon and embroidery thread
- 50 cm bias binding

Complete Steps 1–6 as above, using ribbon stitch, French knots and straight stitch for the flower design.
7. Place outer panel on top of lining with wrong sides together. Tack.
8. Carefully stitch bias binding on right side, hard against piping. Turn to wrong side and slip stitch in place.

actual size

Coat hanger *(piped in green)*

I have a beautiful old early Victorian Sèvres bowl which at some point of its life has been broken and carefully glued together. Obviously its previous owner loved the charming floral design, as I do.

China is a wonderful source for designs, but sometimes you have to adapt the design a little as it can look unbalanced on a flat surface.

Materials

- 25 cm of 112-cm fabric
- 1 m purchased piping or self-made piping cord
- wooden coat hanger
- 15 cm plastic tubing
- silk ribbon (various lengths) — green, cream, 3 shades of pink, mid blue, mid yellow
- 25 cm *pellen*
- a piece of *batting* 45 cm x 10 cm
- embroidery thread (various shades)

1. Use pattern on page 29 to cut out front and back in both fabric and pellen.
2. Transfer design above to the right side of front piece.
3. Tack pellen pieces to wrong side of back and front.
4. Work design in silk ribbon. When complete, wash according to instructions on page 5.
5. Fold batting in half lengthwise, insert hook of hanger through centre of batting. Trim to shape and handstitch cut edges together using large slip stitch. Do not pull the batting tightly or you will lose the bounce of the padding.
6. Insert plastic tubing over metal hook and trim to fit.
7. Using leftover fabric, cut a piece on the cross 4 cm wide and 16 cm long, fold in half with wrong sides together, and stitch along one short end and 14 cm down long side (leaving 2-cm opening).
8. Gently turn through, forming a tube.

9. Put tube over plastic-covered hook. Stitch flaps at end of tube to batting.
10. Apply piping to right side of front piece, starting stitching at point marked on pattern, leaving a tag of piping 1 cm long at beginning. Also leave 1-cm tag at end of stitching. These tags are later tucked down into padding to give a very neat finish to your work.

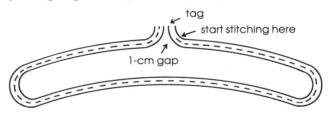

11. With right sides of outer fabric together, and using the previous stitching line as a guide, carefully stitch according to diagram.

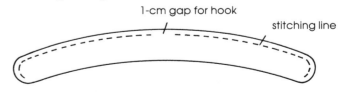

12. Now turn through, insert hook through central hole and bring fabric down over ends. Carefully turn open end in, pin together and handstitch carefully. Attach a small bow at neck of coat hanger if wanted.

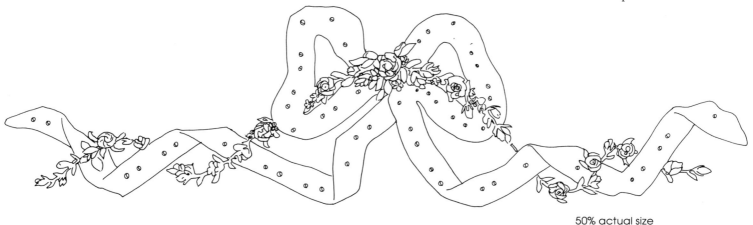

50% actual size

*C*oat hanger *(with bow)*

The bow design used here, and also on the eye shades and toilet bag, was inspired by a lovely bow pattern on the copper cover over the small fireplace in the bedroom of our Edwardian home. I then added the trail of flowers based on old postcards from that era.

Materials

- 35 cm of 112-cm wide fabric
- 1.3 m *beading lace*
- 90 cm *edging lace*
- silk ribbon — 3 shades of pink, mid blue, sharp green
- silk ribbon — 1.3 m pale blue for threading through lace

- 25 cm *pellen*
- *batting* 45 cm x 10 cm
- 15 cm plastic tubing
- embroidery thread
- 75 cm piping

1. Use pattern on page 29 and cut out front and back in both fabric and pellen.
2. Transfer bow design (above) on to right side of one fabric piece.
3. Tack pellen to wrong sides of both pieces of fabric.
4. Shape beading lace according to design: flip the lace in the tails and shape the bow. (These techniques are explained in the heirloom technique section, page 8.) Thread the silk ribbon through the beading lace. Secure the ribbon in place with French knots, using an embroidery thread. Attach the bow with a small zigzag stitch.

5. Now work silk ribbon design. I put in trails of stems and leaves in embroidery thread first and then place the silk ribbon roses (stitches to use on pages 6–7).
6. Wash fabric and dry as instructed on page 5.
7. Cover hook and apply piping as described in steps 5 to 9 in instructions for the coat hanger with piping (opposite).
8. Turn base edge under 2 cm and butt lace to folded edge. Stitch into place using a small zigzag stitch. Stitch hem again 2 cm above previous row of stitching.

Spectacles case *(Design 1)*

This very simple design came from a book about the American Amish people. I made it a little smaller to accommodate my half-glasses.

Materials

- 20 x 23 cm piece of fabric
- 7 x 20 cm piece of fabric
- 20 x 23 cm piece of *pellen*
- silk ribbon — blue, gold

- 23 cm square of satin lining
- green embroidery thread
- blue sewing thread

1. Using a marker pen, transfer the trellis design on this page onto the large piece of fabric. Using a twin needle on your machine, pintuck trellis design, being careful not to stretch the fabric.

2. Take the 7 x 20 cm strip of fabric. Leaving a margin of 1 cm, pintuck lengthwise over 2.5 cm width (approximately 6–7 rows), leaving a remaining 3.5 cm plain for facing. Using first row of pintucking as guide, turn under 1-cm seam allowance.

3. Wash larger piece of fabric to remove markings. Zigzag pellen to wrong side of fabric.

4. Embroider flower designs using straight stitch, French knots and stem stitch (see The Stitches on pages 6–7), placing as desired.

5. Place folded edge of pintucked strip, with right side facing, on right side of embroidered piece, 1 cm down from top edge. Topstitch, using pintuck line as guide.

6. With right sides together, stitch lining to facing strip with a 1 cm seam.

7. Open out so lining is free of embroidered piece. Fold in half lengthwise with right sides together. Starting at base, stitch seam along base, up long side and across other short end, leaving a 5-cm opening on long side for turning through.

8. Using this gap, pull right side through. Hand stitch the opening. Now push lining to the inside and gently press.

actual size

Spectacles case *(Design 2)*

actual size

Materials

- 16 x 25 cm piece of fabric
- 4 x 20 cm piece of fabric
- 5 x 20 cm piece of fabric
- 16 x 25 cm piece of *pellen*
- 16 x 25 cm piece of satin lining
- 2 x 20 cm strip of piping
- eyeglass case frames
- bias binding for embroidery

1. Take 16 x 25 cm oblong of fabric and using the short edge as a guide, pintuck completely across the fabric. Recut this piece to measure 15 x 20 cm. This allows for any distortion.

2. Pintuck in rows lengthwise the 4 x 20 cm strip to go at bottom of case (approximately 4 rows). The first row should be 2 cm from the cut edge .

3. Pintuck in rows lengthwise the 5 x 20 cm strip to go at top of case (approximately 6 rows). Again, the first row should be 2 cm from cut edge. Press all pieces on the wrong side.

4. With raw edges matching, attach piping to top and bottom edges of large piece of fabric.

5. With right sides together, put 2 cm plain edge of 4 x 20 cm strip to edge of centre panel, and sew with a 1-cm seam using the stitch line of piping as your guide. Apply top strip in the same way.

6. Cut piece of pellen to the same size as assembled case and attach to wrong side of fabric with zigzag stitch.

7. Fold fabric in half to give back and front, and mark centre of front piece. Work silk ribbon design (in spider web roses, straight stitch, ribbon stitch and French knots, see pages 6–7) centred on this point.

8. Cut the lining fabric so it is 1 cm shorter in length than the outer fabric. With right sides together, stitch lining to outer fabric 1 cm from top edge. Open out and topstitch lining to seam allowance.

9. To make casing for eyeglass frames, take bias binding and place on wrong side of outer fabric, covering 2nd, 3rd and 4th rows of pintucking up from piping. Tack in place. On right side stitch along 2nd and 5th rows of pintucking. Insert eyeglass frames, one from each end.

10. Follow steps 7 and 8 in previous instructions to complete.

*L*avender bags

These always make wonderful gifts. Inspiration for these designs came from a piece of china — the roses from a dear little Victorian coffee cup — a Victorian postcard inspired the golden cherub, and lily of the valley has always been a great favourite both now and in the past.

Lily of the Valley design

Materials

- 16 x 25 cm fabric
- 16 x 25 cm satin
- 60 cm *insertion lace*
- 25 cm *beading lace*
- 25 cm 6-cm wide *edging lace*
- 1.25 m 7-mm wide silk ribbon for beading lace
- 7-mm wide silk ribbon — green, white
- green embroidery thread
- 25 cm *entredeux*

actual size

1. Fold fabric in half to give front and back.
2. Using design above, transfer design and shape of lace oval onto front fabric piece.
3. Shape lace (see pages 8–9).
4. Attach lace using a small zigzag stitch.
5. Work silk ribbon design in ribbon stitch, French knots and stem stitch.
6. Attach entredeux across top using stitch in ditch and roll and whip (see page 8).
7. Trim away waste from entredeux and add insertion lace (lace to entredeux method, see page 8).
8. Add beading lace to insertion lace (lace to lace method, see page 8) and then wide lace.
9. Fold fabric in half and stitch across base and up side, including lace.
10. Thread ribbon through beading lace.
11. Fold satin lining in half with right sides together.
12. Stitch around base, side and top, leaving a 5-cm gap.
13. Turn through, and fill with lavender. Hand stitch opening.
14. Place in lavender bag and tie ribbon with a bow in centre front.

Opposite top: A beautiful early Victorian Sèvres bowl inspired the floral designs on these coat hangers, while the bow design came from a copper cover on a bedroom fireplace.
Opposite bottom: The hussif is basically a needleworker's tool kit and can be as elaborate as you wish. I designed this one for silk ribbon work. Another decorative and practical project is the heart-shaped pincushion.

Above: This viola motif was adapted from an 18th-century book on silk fabric designs.

Left: The bow, repeated and adapted, and two lovely lavender bags.

Below: A spectacles case featuring a garland of flowers, taken from an old book of poems.

Opposite top left: This gorgeous silk satin nightgown is made using heirloom sewing techniques.

Opposite top right: Bodice detail of the nightgown.

Opposite bottom: Cheerful padded tea cosies were popular in Edwardian times.

Above: Colonial crafts make charming gifts. Here are two eye shades, a spectacles case and a lavender bag.
Left: Flowers have always been popular as the basis for needlework designs and many were featured on pillows and cushions, used in abundance on beds and chairs in years gone by.
Below: This fantasy flower cushion is the pinnacle of the silk ribbon worker's art.

Roses design actual size

Materials

- 15 x 22 cm linen or similar fabric
- 13 x 22 cm satin
- 22 cm *entredeux*
- 22 cm *insertion lace*
- 22 cm *beading lace*
- 22 cm wide e*dging lace*
- 1 m 4-mm wide silk ribbon
- silk ribbon — 3 shades of pink, sharp green

1. Stitch pintucks across fabric leaving 3.5 cm for the rose design.
2. Follow Steps 6–10 as in Lily of the Valley design.
3. To make satin inner, follow steps 11–14, using smaller measurements as shown in requirements.
4. Work silk ribbon stitch and your preferred rose stitch on front (see pages 6–7).

Cherub design

Materials

- 2 pieces linen or similar fabric, 12 x 15 cm
- Small brass cherub
- 30 cm insertion lace
- 1 m edging lace
- 2 pieces 10 cm x 12 cm satin
- silk ribbon for embroidery (in your choice of colours)
- gold thread

1. Transfer same pattern for placement of lace from Lily of the Valley design and shape lace, placing outer edge of lace on traced line. Zigzag in place.
2. Using gold thread, stitch cherub in centre.
3. Using silk ribbon, work design in lazy daisy stitch, French knots, ribbon stitch and fly stitch (see pages 8–9).
4. Gather edging lace by pulling thread on straight edge.
5. Using a zigzag stitch, attach lace around outer edge of shaped lace.
6. Fold lace over towards cherub and tack lightly. This will stop it getting caught in seam.
7. With right sides together, front on top, stitch around shape, 5 mm outside lace stitching line and leaving a 6-cm gap for turning through.
8. Trim away excess fabric, leaving a 5-mm edge. Clip curves.
9. Turn through. Remove tacking thread in lace.
10. Cut out satin inner using pattern piece. Stitch, with wrong sides together, leaving a 4-cm gap. Turn through gap, fill with lavender and close by hand.
12. Insert satin inner through side hole of cover and hand stitch together.

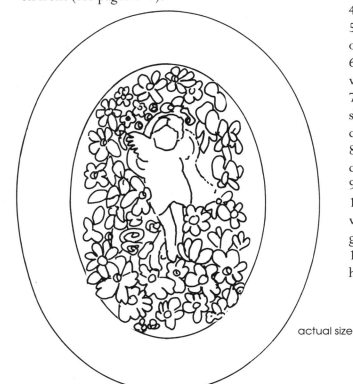

actual size

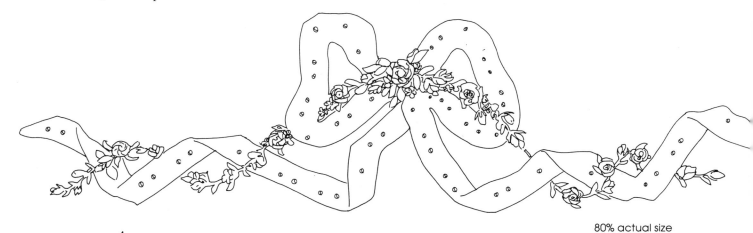

80% actual size

Toilet bag

Our ancestors were very fond of round boxes, hence the shape of this very practical item, again utilising the bow design seen in the coathanger.

Materials

- *Swiss batiste*
  main colour: 24 x 57 cm for side
  19 cm diameter circle for lid
  5 x 37 cm for handle
  second colour: 16 x 57 cm for side
  2 x 19-cm diameter circles
  5 x 37 cm for handle
- 2.5 m *beading lace*
- 2.5 m ribbon
- piping

- 46-cm long zip
- silk ribbon — 3 tones of pink, mid blue, sharp green
- embroidery thread — sharp green, to match ribbon
- 2 circles of lightweight plastic 17 cm diameter
- *pellen*, 2 x 20-cm diameter circles
- calico, 2 x 20-cm diameter circles
- interfacing, 10 x 37 cm
- Parka nylon: 2 x 19-cm diameter circles
  14 x 57 cm for pouches
  15 x 57 cm for lining

NB: I used Swiss batiste to match a nightgown using the same design, and used it double because it is so fine. If you are using a thicker fabric, a single thickness will do.

1. Fold larger piece of fabric in main colour in half, press and tack raw edges together.
2. Fold larger piece of fabric in second colour in half, press and tack raw edges together.
3. Using the large bow pattern (above), trace design onto main fabric making sure that bottom of design does not go below edge of fabric. When centring lace on design you will find that on ribbons the lace is flipped and on bows the lace is shaped. Pin lace to fabric, placing pins across lace. When all shaping is done, lightly spray with starch and leave to dry. Using a small zigzag, carefully stitch around the top of the design and on the inside of the bow. Do not stitch around the bottom of design. Do not go across lace.
4. Cut away fabric along bottom edge to within 0.5 cm of stitched lace. Do not cut inside bows.
5. Place lace bows over the top edge of second colour, making sure fabric edge is level with middle of bow. Pin in place and lightly spray with starch and leave to dry. Zigzag along bottom edge of lace.

6. **Base** — Take both circles of second colour (if using lightweight fabric, see note previously), 1 circle of pellen and 1 circle of calico. Put first calico, then pellen and, finally, 2 circles of second colour on top. Now machine-quilt all together with a square 3-cm grid.

7. Take 1 circle of plastic and 1 circle of inside lining material. Put plastic on inner side of quilted fabric and then lining material on top. Tack all together and complete, enclosing plastic.

8. **Sides** — Sew ends of sides together and then divide and mark 0.5 cm and 1 cm division.

9. Take lining 14 x 57 cm and neaten with machine along both long sides. Place this on larger piece of lining and divide to make pockets. Machine stitch divisions. Sew ends together. Tack lining inside outer fabric, matching seams.

10. Divide and mark quarters on base and then, with right sides together, pin and machine stitch side to base.

11. Fold zip in half, top to bottom and centre on middle of upper edge of bag. Pin in place and stitch.

12. **Lid** — Take remaining circle of calico, pellen and lining fabric. Mark small bow pattern (see page 32) onto circle of main colour. Tack around circumference to circle of pellen. Then attach lace and work embroidery.

13. **Handle** — Interface each piece of handle material (both colours). Thread ribbon through beading and centre this on top layer of handle. Zigzag to attach. Work French knots to anchor ribbon.

14. Attach piping to each side of main colour strip. Put right sides together and, using previous line of stitching as guide, stitch both pieces together. Pull through.

15. Using 0.5 cm markings as your guide on lid, stitch handle to right side of lid with raw edges together, making sure the bow is facing the front to match bow on side.

16. Take piping in second colour and attach to outer edge of circle, going over the handle.

17. Match back seam on side piece with back quarter mark on lid. With right sides together pin lid and sides together between start and end of zip.

18. Turn bag inside out. Using markings as your guide, pin zip to remaining section of lid; open zip, tack and stitch. Turn through once more.

19. Flatten zip inwards. Insert plastic circle so seams are on top of plastic. This ensures seam allowances do not show on outside of lid. Take circle of parka nylon and run a gathering thread 1 cm in from edge. Gather up slightly and press inwards. Attach to lid by hand, covering plastic circle and seam allowance.

Tea cosy

Thick padded tea cosies were especially popular in Edwardian times and an embroidered cover was often placed over the tea cosy. It could then easily be removed for washing. This particular design was taken from one of these covers found amongst some old linen.

Materials

- 2 pieces of linen/cotton mixture 35 x 35 cm
- *pellen*, 2 pieces 30 x 35 cm
- *batting*, 1 piece 30 x 35 cm
- lining, 2 pieces 30 x 35 cm
- 75 cm piping
- silk ribbon — 7-mm wide gold, green, cream, beige, camel; 4-mm widegold
- embroidery thread — beige, green

1. Using pattern on page 32, cut 2 shapes each in outer fabric, pellen, lining and batting (but cut batting and lining shorter as indicated on the pattern).

2. Transfer design (page 30) to front.

3. Pin pellen to wrong side of outer fabric on front and back pieces, and zigzag together.

4. Machine-quilt the back at 5-cm intervals. Also join batting to lining and machine-quilt together at 50-cm intervals.

5. Work design on front in ribbon stitch, stem stitch, straight stitch, pistil stitch and French knots (see pages 6–7) in silk ribbon and embroidery thread. Also put ribbon across back to match front fabric, attaching with French knots.

6. Machine piping to front pieces.

7. **Loop** — Cut a 10 x 4 cm piece from leftover fabric. Stitch 1-cm seam lengthwise and turn through. Decorate if desired. Fold in half and stitch at centre top of cosy over piping, with raw edges together.

8. Join front and back pieces to lining pieces across base.

9. Putting right sides together, stitch around outside of both leaving an 8-cm gap for turning out.

10. Trim away the excess batting and clip curved seam allowances.

11. Pull through to right side and carefully stitch the 8-cm opening by hand.

Blouse

I was browsing through a book I have on silk designs for fabrics of the 18th century and was taken by a lovely design of violas, which, with a lot of adaptation, became the design for this blouse. The sleeve pattern is a simplified version and I have used very strong colours, as was popular at that time.

Materials

- simple blouse pattern
- linen fabric as per pattern
- 3 m *entredeux*
- silk ribbon — 7-mm wide ribbon for lower petals; 4-mm ribbon for top petals (2 colours)
- embroidery thread — green, yellow
- enough iron-on interfacing for neck facing and 2 x 2.5-cm strips to go round sleeves

actual size

1. Cut out back and sleeves from blouse pattern.
2. Measure length of front from highest point of shoulder seam and using this measurement for length, cut 3 strips of fabric 7 cm wide. To the back of one of these, interface with an iron-on fusing. Embroider this strip in straight stitch for petals and stem stitch and French knots (see pages 6–7).
3. Pintuck 4 strips of fabric, measured length 4 cm wide, with 3 rows, making sure they are centred.
4. Add entredeux to each side of pintucked strips. (Stitch in ditch, roll and whip methods, see page 8).

5. Join all strips together as in diagram.
6. Place purchased pattern front on joined centre piece and estimate how wide each side panel needs to be, adding an extra 2 cm to both sides. Join and once more place pattern on material.
7. Cut out front.
8. **Sleeves** — Using hem fold line as guide, do a row of pintucking. Do a further 2 rows above this row. Leaving a space of 2.5 cm, do another 3 rows of pintucks. Cut a strip of iron-on interfacing 2.5 cm wide and apply between the two sets of pintucks. Work embroidery in this space as above.
9. Make up blouse in usual way.

(The blouse shown in the colour section has an opening on the shoulder, but this pattern can easily accommodate an opening in the back.)

pintucked	plain panel	pintucked	centre panel	pintucked	embroidered panel	pintucked

S ilk nightgown

Beautiful nightgowns have always been loved by women. This simple gown is made in silk satin using heirloom techniques — it could well have been worn by our forebears.

Materials

- silk — 1 piece full width x length from bust to required length (for skirt, A); 1 piece full width x ¼ of the above measurement (for front panel); 1 piece full width x 30 cm (for yoke)
- 6.5 m cotton *insertion lace*
- 4 m 7-cm wide cotton *edging lace*
- 4 m 13-mm ribbon
- *entredeux*
- 20 x 30 cm lining
- silk ribbon for embroidery
- silk embroidery thread

1. Start with skirt section. Cut off selvedges carefully. (I pull a thread to be quite sure it is straight.) With right sides together, attach entredeux to edges from which selvedges have been removed (stitch in ditch and roll and whip, see page 8).

2. Using lace to entredeux technique (see page 8), attach lace to entredeux then attach ribbon, then another length of lace.

Centre panel

3. Divide material for front panel into 4 equal parts, having first removed selvedges.

4. Across the end of each piece, add a length of ribbon and a piece of lace. Above the ribbon put 8 rows of pintucks from side to side.

5. Overlap lace over top of next panel and pin. Check length against A. Each section may have to be shortened

pintucking
ribbon
lace

slightly, depending on the width of the lace used. Once the combined length of all four sections is the same as A, apply lace of fabric using a small zigzag stitch following edge of lace.

6. Attach entredeux down combined length of central panel on both sides. Join A to central point using lace to entredeux techniques (see page 8).

Hem

7. Attach entredeux around hem line (stitch in ditch, roll and whip, see page 8). Trim away waste on entredeux. Then attach wide lace, gathering only very slightly.

Armholes

8. Putting skirt wrong sides together, cut out armholes as per diagram. Roll armhole edges and either hand or machine stitch.

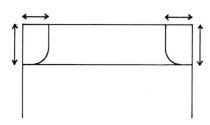

Yoke

9. Using a basic yoke pattern as a guide, make a paper pattern like this.

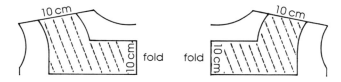

Fold fabric as shown, cut 1 of each. Also cut out lining. Stitch shoulder seams.

10. Shape lace around yoke, mitring corners and shoulder, putting straight side of lace on outside edge and allowing for seam allowance. Stitch. Embroider design over mitred seams. Join yoke and lining together.

11. Stitch yoke to skirt in normal manner. Hand stitch bottom of lining in place.

12. Stitch ribbon to outer edge of yoke.

$\mathcal{H}$uss i f *for silk ribbon work*

The idea of a hussif is a very old one, and is in fact a shortening of the word 'housewife'. Over the years, it has taken many forms, from elaborate embroidered hussifs to very simple ones given to soldiers as part of their kit when they went to war. Basically it is a roll containing needles, pins, scissors, tape measure, threads, etc.

Because I teach silk ribbon embroidery, I wanted a roll which would contain the items I needed. What is different from normal is that it has tubes to hold a wash-away marker pen and a pencil. Also the pin cushion usually present has been replaced by a small pocket as I rarely use pins.

Materials
- outer fabric: an oblong of fabric 40 x 25 cm
- inner fabric: 30 cm of fabric 115 cm wide
- *pellen* 40 x 25 cm
- 1.1 m *insertion lace*
- 30 cm medium-weight iron-on interfacing
- 2 x 18-cm zips
- silk ribbon: 3 shades of same colour and green for leaves
- embroidery thread for stems
- fabric for binding (or 90 cm bias binding)
- 1.2 m piping
- 10 cm flannel or felt

Outer
1. Pull a thread near the edge of the fabric to ensure a straight line, then cut an oblong of fabric 40 x 25 cm. Fold in half, short side to short side. Finger press and, using this line as your guide, pintuck the entire piece of fabric. Press on wrong side, pulling into shape if necessary.
2. Place wrong side of fabric on pellen, then cut to shape using the pattern on page 31. Pin carefully together and zigzag all the way around.
3. Shape lace all the way around according to pattern, leaving a 1.5-cm band between lace and edge of fabric.

4. Using a small zigzag, stitch lace to fabric. Work small rose design in oval (see page 10, or use the stitches on pages 6–7).

Inner
5. Cut a piece of fabric 12 x 23 cm for the centre panel.
6. Cut two pieces of fabric 30 x 23 cm long for the side panels.
7. Cut one piece of fabric 25 x 30 cm. This piece is for all the pockets and tubes. Back each piece with interfacing.

Pencil and pen tubes

8. Fold an oblong piece of fabric, approximately 6 x 30 cm, in half, short end to short end. Wrap fabric around pencil to check size. Stitch across short end. Turn inside. Now lay either side of 23-cm side of middle section. Put pencil or marker pen inside to check position before stitching. Zip will lie on top of this.

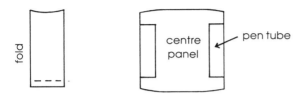

Centre panel

9. Putting right sides together, line up edge of zip to 23-cm length of centre panel. This gives a sandwich of the centre panel, pencil tube and zip with the wrong side uppermost. Stitch using zipper foot and then turn under.
10. Take one side panel and fold as per diagram. This forms pocket.

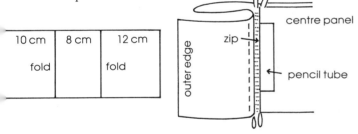

This edge is now placed on top of other side of zip and stitched carefully by hand. The fabric should butt against central panel, completely covering zip. Reverse positioning to make pocket at other end.

Embroidered pockets

11. Using shapes on main pattern, carefully cut 4 pieces of fabric. Embroider front of 2 large pieces (scissors and needle cases), remembering to reverse pattern.
12. Using third colour, stitch piping to right side of both fronts. With right sides together, stitch back and front, carefully following line established by piping, leaving a 4-cm gap at side to be able to pull through. Clip edges. Pull through and hand stitch opening.
13. Do the same for the pin case and tape measure case.
14. Position scissor case in place and very carefully hand stitch along piping line to top layer of side panel (not through pocket), leaving a 6-cm opening at top for scissors. If you open the zip, this is quite easily done and avoids the mistake of sewing all three layers of zippered pocket.

Needle and pin flaps

15. Stitch 3 cm across top of both to create flaps. Cut 2 small shapes of flannel for the pin flap on the centre panel and 4 larger shapes for the needle case on the side panel (cutting slightly smaller than the case pattern size). Embroider around the edges of flannel shapes with buttonhole sititch, either on the machine or by hand. Stitch to appropriate panels.

Tape measure case

16. Stitch along piping line, leaving a 7-cm opening.

Pin case

17. Stitch to centre panel 4 cm across top.

18. Mark position for buttons and stitch in place (you may like to put a button underneath for strength). Again take care not to stitch through pocket. Make button loop by buttonhole stitching over several loops of embroidery or chainstitch loop.
19. Place inner on top of outer cover, wrong sides together. Tack in place. Cut binding for outer edge 5-cm wide on the cross. (Join to get length required if necessary.) Fold in half and tack raw edges together. Line up cut edge of binding with outer edge of hussif. Stitch on right side of outer, lining outer edge of machine foot to outside edge. Turn binding to inside and stitch in place by hand.
20. Fold hussif into thirds. Put button at side and make loop (as above) to fasten.

$\mathcal{F}$antasy flower cushion

The design for this cushion was suggested by a small Sevrès porcelain plaque on a piece of furniture in the Wallace Collection in London. While I have heavily adapted the floral section, the base is very similar.

I started doing fantasy flowers when I was asked if I would take a class with a male in it who 'didn't want to do little roses and forget-me-nots'!! I have really enjoyed using the 7-mm wide silk ribbon because of the wonderful 3-dimensional effects one can get. Suddenly I am able to reproduce the charming still-life pictures the Edwardians used to love to do.

Use the picture in the colour section as a guide and add colours to suit your taste. You can embroider the flowers in a variety of stitches, and I am sure you will invent some of your own. I have used roses, violas, irises, fuchsias, marigolds, daisies, delphiniums and wheat. The pattern can be transferred onto your fabric or used as a guide only.

On completion, make up the cushion as desired, remembering to carefully wash your embroidery first (see instructions on page 5). The one in the colour section has a border of silk.

60% actual size

Pillow

Beautiful pillows were used in abundance on beds and chairs in years gone by. Flowers were always a popular theme. This pillow, illustrated in the colour section, is another design to use as your imagination takes you. I became very excited doing this pillow and just added to it as the mood took me. You can add as much or as little as you want, working in the colours of your choice. Use the coloured picture and pattern as guides. I have worked roses, rose buds, daisies, fuchsias, forget-me-nots, irises, hollyhocks, flannel flowers and wisteria. Have fun!

80% actual size

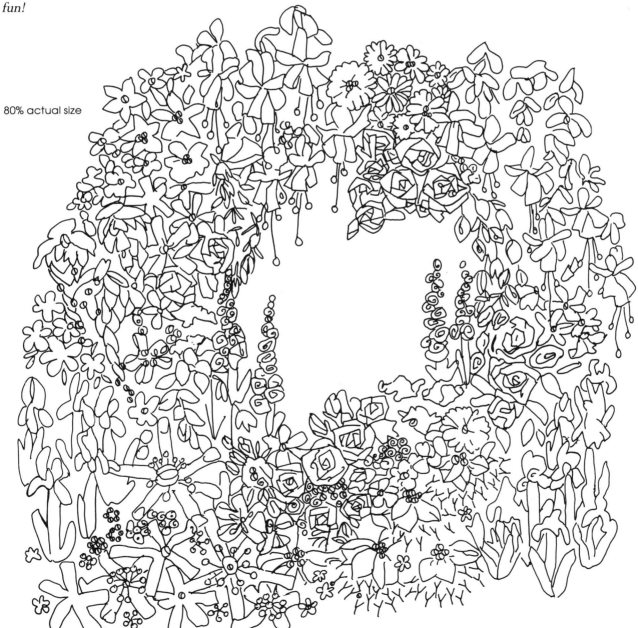

The patterns

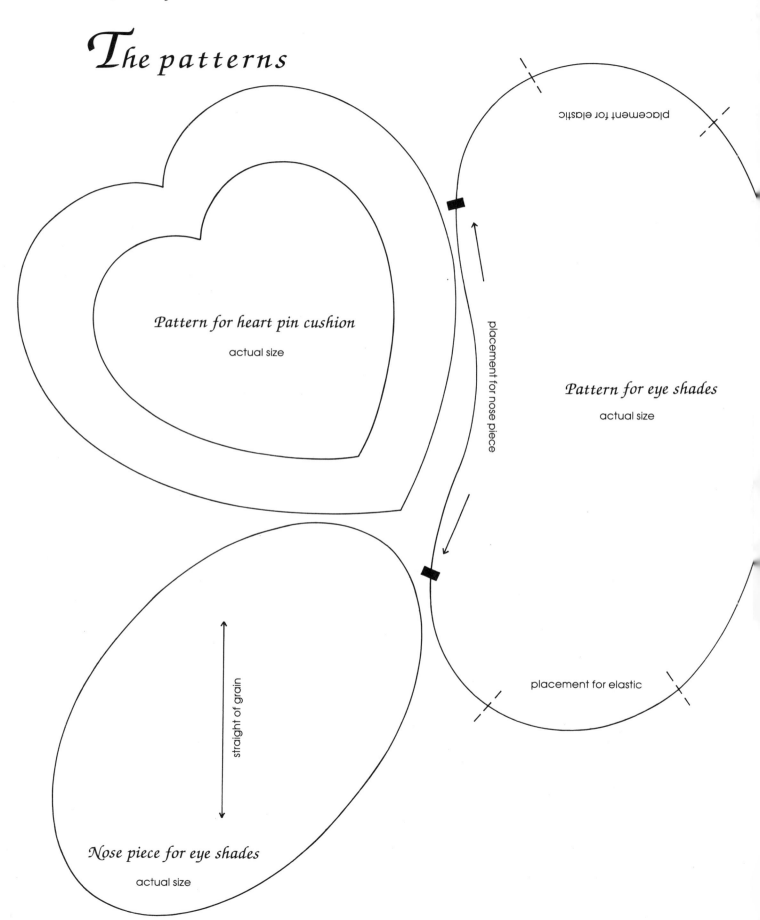

Pattern for heart pin cushion

actual size

placement for elastic

Pattern for eye shades

actual size

placement for nose piece

straight of grain

Nose piece for eye shades

actual size

placement for elastic

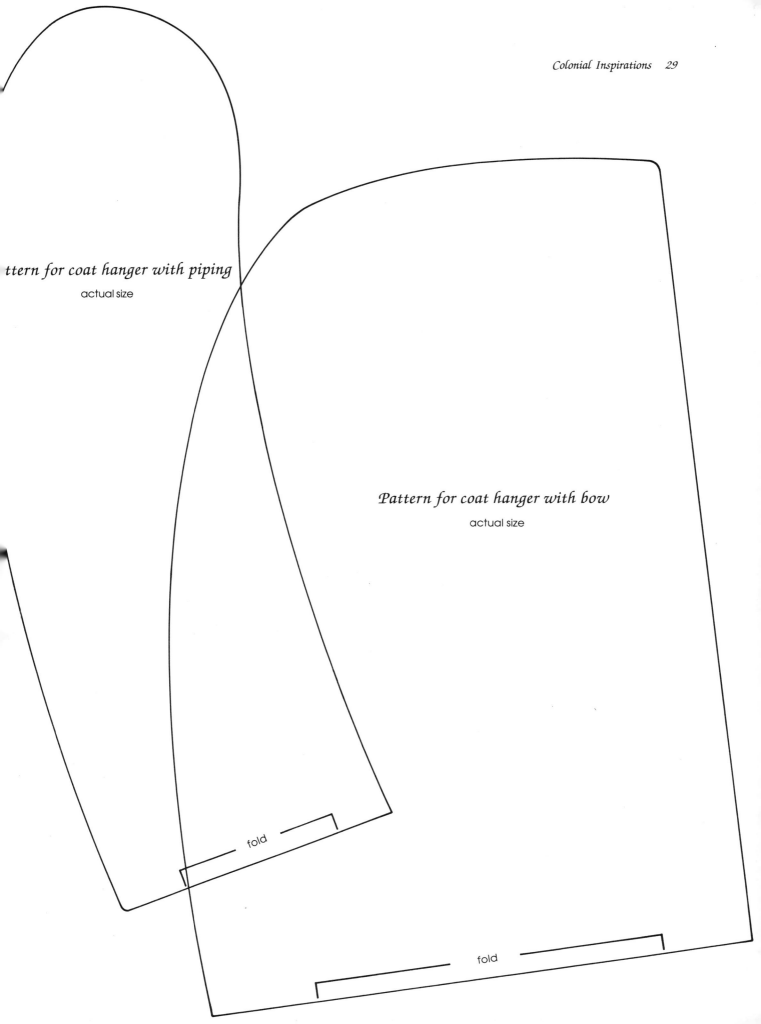

ttern for coat hanger with piping

actual size

Pattern for coat hanger with bow

actual size

fold

fold

Pattern for tea cosy

80% actual size

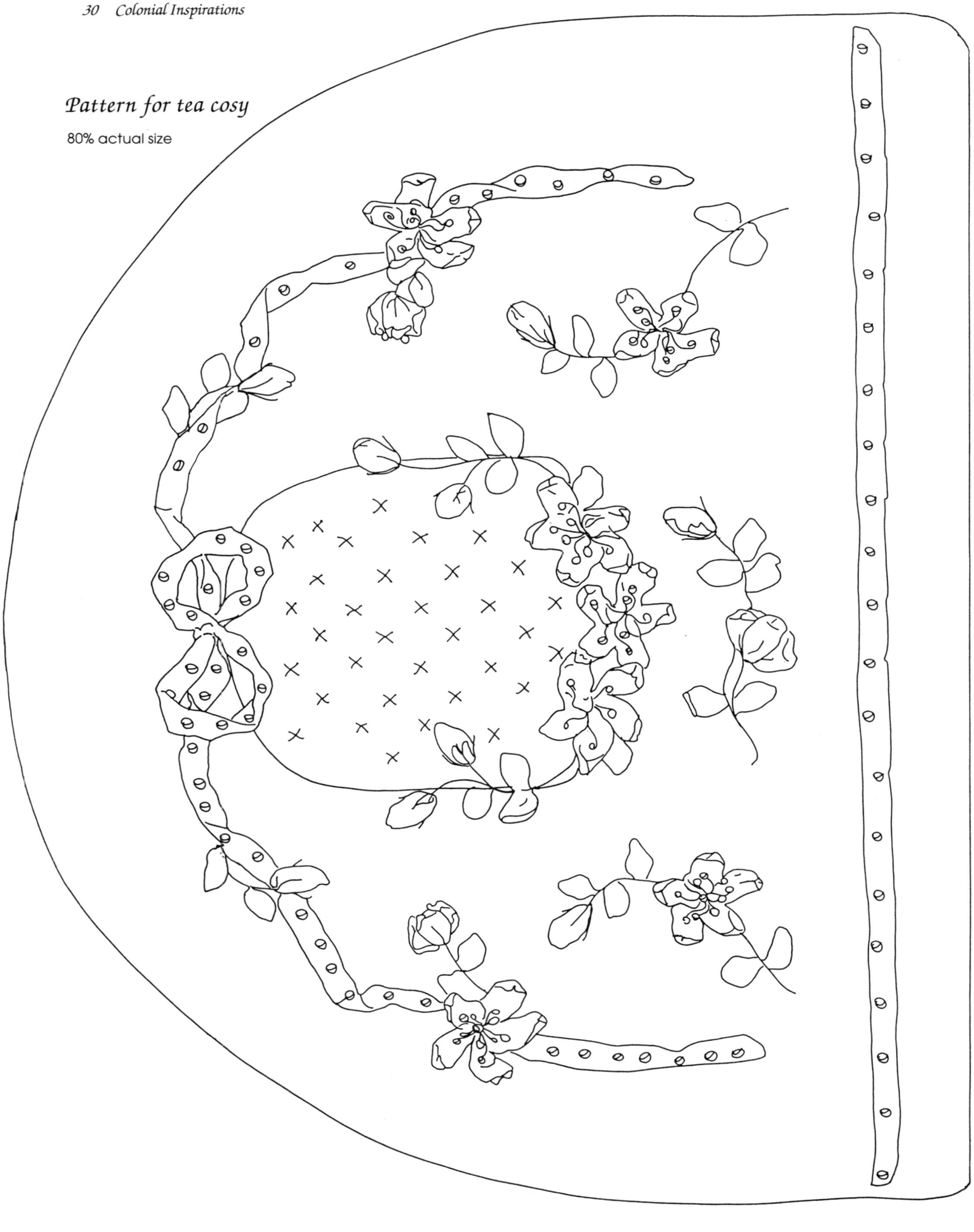

Pattern for hussif

80% actual size

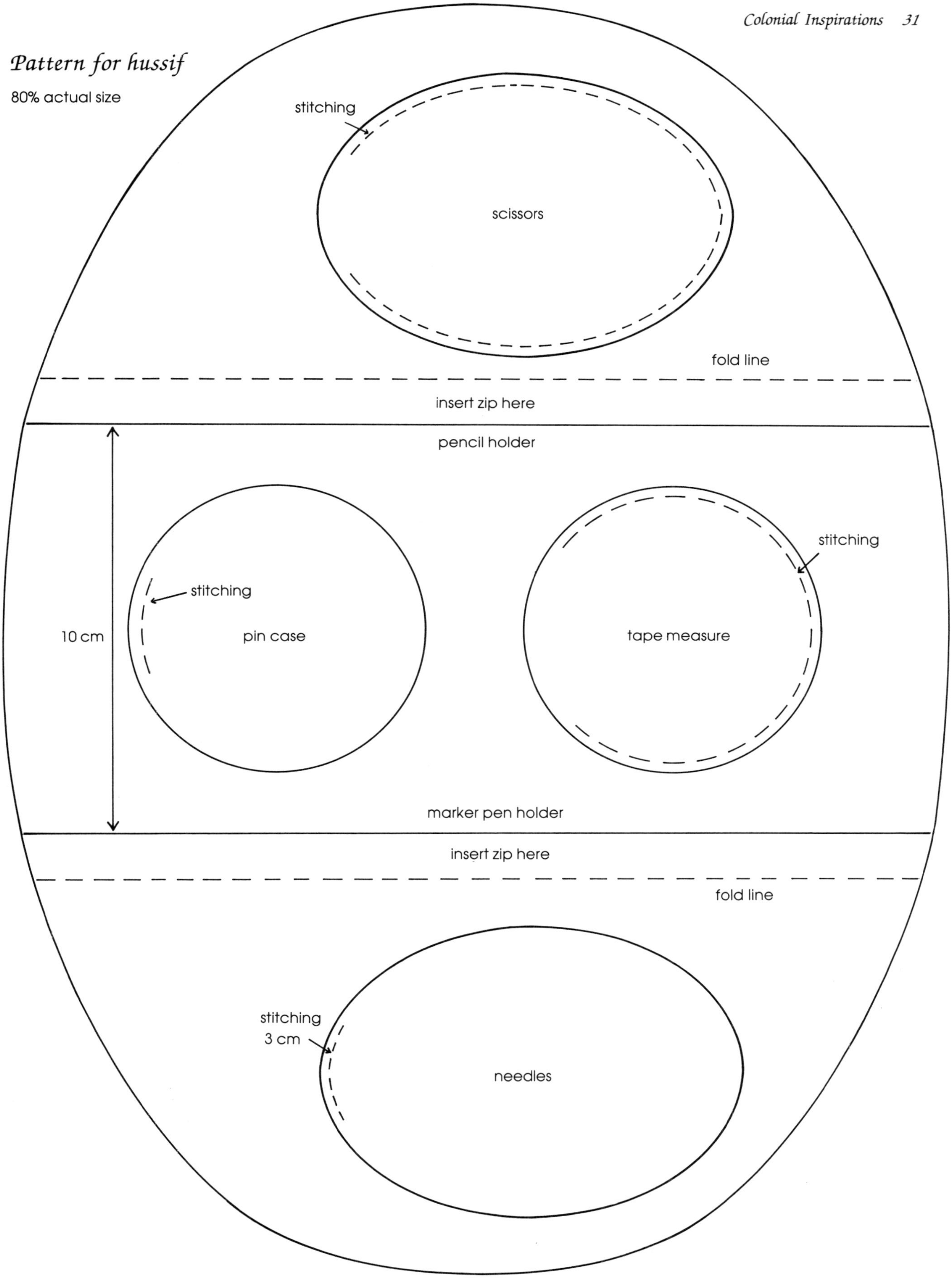

stitching

scissors

fold line

insert zip here

pencil holder

stitching

pin case

stitching

tape measure

10 cm

marker pen holder

insert zip here

fold line

stitching
3 cm

needles

Bow design

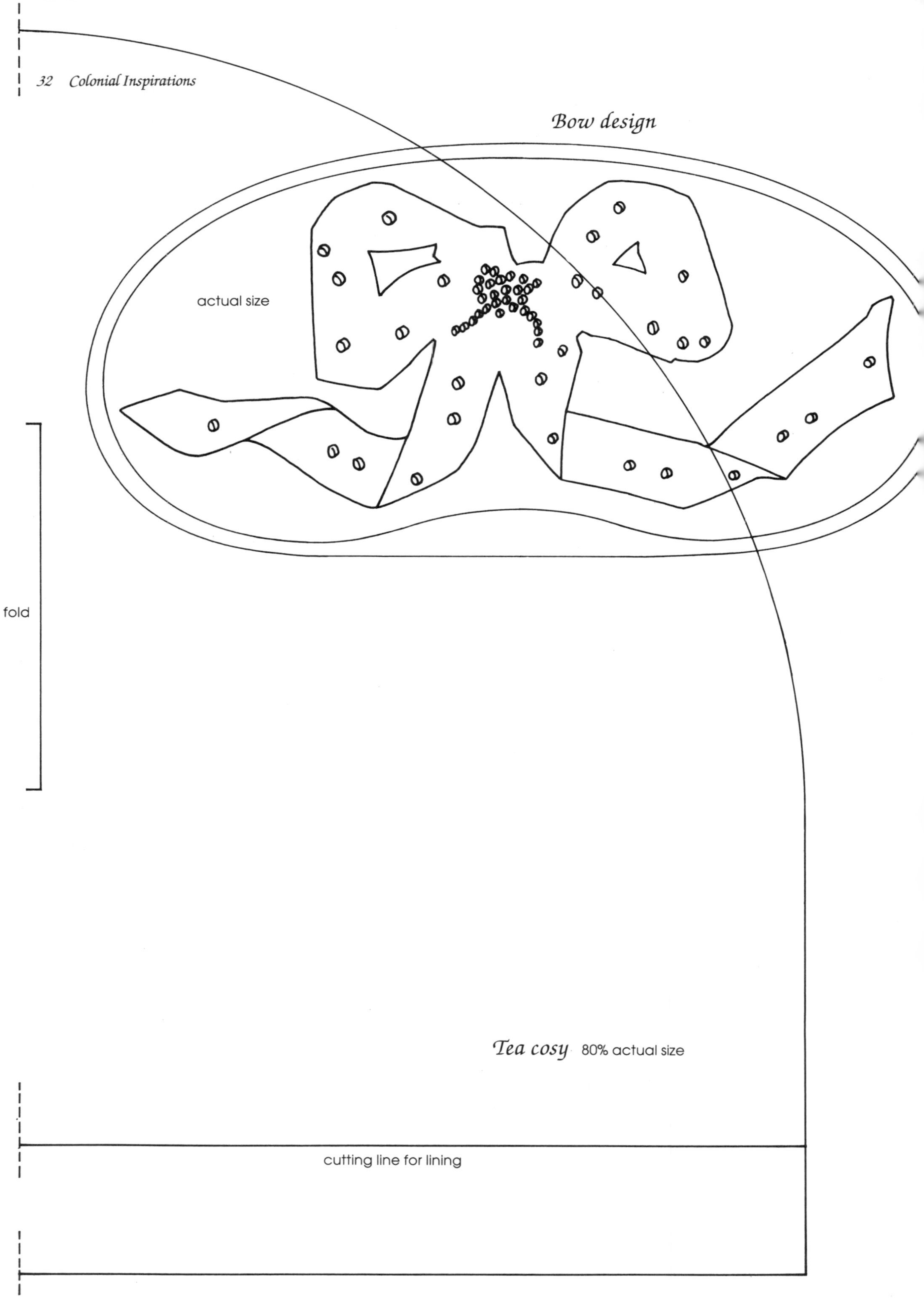

actual size

fold

Tea cosy 80% actual size

cutting line for lining